Hack the Corporate Ladder

BY ROBERT T. GOFOURTH

ROBERT T. GOFOURTH

©2017 Robert T. Gofourth
Durham N.C. 27701

Publisher:
Elite Online Publishing
63 East 11400 South
Suite #230
Sandy, UT 84070
info@EliteOnlinePublishing.com

ALL RIGHTS RESERVED. This book contains material protected under International and Federal Copyright Laws and Treaties. Any unauthorized reprint or use of this material is prohibited. No part of this book may be reproduced or transmitted in any form or by any means electronic or mechanical including photocopying, recording, or by any information storage and retrieval system without express written permission from the author/publisher.

ISBN-13: 978-1536912937
ISBN-10: 153691293X

DEDICATION

This book is dedicated...

To all of the hard working people around the World. It is human nature to strive to do the best we can and to contribute in a meaningful way.

To all of the frontline employees – your work is important and has a positive impact on your company and the people you serve. Your effort has purpose.

To all leaders no matter your title, remember that leadership is serious business. Your employees depend on to guide and develop them. Your leadership is needed more than ever. Thank you for your LEADERSHIP!

ROBERT T. GOFOURTH

TABLE OF CONTENTS

Acknowledgments 1

Forward 5

Introduction 7

Expect Excellence of Yourself and Others 13

Be Authentically Human…Faults & All 27

Never Lose Sight of Your Priorities 69

Continuous Self-Improvement 87

3-Point Management Philosophy 103

Afterword 107

About The Author 117

ROBERT T. GOFOURTH

ACKNOWLEDGMENTS

First of all, I would like to thank my friends Bill Harris and Murphy D. Bishop, II who were the first to encourage me to write about my professional experiences. To my parents who taught me how to be a valuable contributor to society and have been wonderful guides in my life – I love you all so much. Big kudos to Kate Frank for her collaboration in the various versions of *Hack the Corporate Ladder* and for being a brilliant editor. Dennis Martinez, thanks for bringing me into the 21st century of digital communication and social media! To Miss Eagle Eyes herself, Robin Maher, I think you could find black specs in pepper!

To all of the horrible bosses I have had (you know who you are) thank you for teaching me what not to do. Thank you to all of my wonderful bosses and thank goodness I've had more good ones than bad. Thank you for believing in me, thank you for giving me opportunity and thank you for teaching me. The people whom I owe a great debt of gratitude to are the people who have allowed me to lead them. I hope I was able to do something good along the way for most of you. Those of you who I unfortunately "practiced" on, thank you and in many cases, I'm sorry. And finally, a very special thanks and much gratitude to Wayne Selkirk, you are the best first boss anyone could ever have.

The journey of my professional career has made me the person I am today. It may be viewed as a good journey to some and not so good to others. I was compelled to write this book because not a week goes by that someone doesn't either ask me about employment, to mentor them or simply how they get to the next level. I will tell you, going through the process of writing your first book and particularly a retrospective, is extremely cathartic and honestly humbling. I suspect my current CEO, a wonderful leader named Brad Wilson, was mortified when he and I were doing a panel discussion last year and I told the audience, "I love to tell on myself" and I shared an example of some bad behavior or failure that I had experienced in my own career. However, it is by these stories, examples and experiences that we all grow as people, no matter the topic.

The fact is, every single person reading this book is a leader in some venue. While you may not lead people at work, you may not have children or sit on a board of directors, you are a leader! People are watching you every moment of the day. It maybe someone in your house of worship, your neighbor, your grandchild, your employee or your friend.

I came to this realization by kidding around with my friend Bill whom I mentioned above. I am a numbers guy, I listen to Frank Sinatra (and love streaming recordings off of vinyl because you can hear the scratches) and I simply can't understand why Wolfie's Diner in Miami Beach closed. I'm probably not the coolest guy you will encounter this year! Bill describes me as a racehorse in business but I think he is a racehorse in fashion and pop culture. It's when we were having a discussion around such things I realize every single one of us are leaders in our own realm. I want you to remember that and to pay attention around your sphere of influence. It will be eye opening to you.

I hope you enjoy the book. I hope I have contributed something to your day, even if it's just a smile from reading one of the stories. And remember, you are exactly where you are supposed to be at this moment but the future is an exciting place and I can't wait to get there with each and every one of you.

ROBERT T. GOFOURTH

FORWARD

The moment you pick up this tremendous book, you will hold in your hands a practical guide to gain success in the workplace. This book will enable you to learn from the trials and errors of someone who has been there, done that, and gotten the t-shirt. Well guess what--now you get the t-shirt just by reading this book.

In *Hack the Corporate Ladder,* Rob Gofourth acts as your personal mentor by sharing stories and best practices from his own experience that he wishes he would have known long ago. He gives real, hands-on advice that you can apply to your position right now--in real time. While reading this book, you can make a list of action items and hit the ground running to make progress in your career.

I recommend this book to anyone who wants to fast-track their career, make an impact in their organization, and shorten the learning curve while doing so. Thanks to Rob, you don't have to reinvent the wheel by repeating his mistakes. Take the wheel that is this book and get yourself rolling toward success!

-Simon T. Bailey

Leader of the Brilliance Movement

Simon T. Bailey International, Inc.

INTRODUCTION

How to Read and Use This Book

Imagine for a moment you have achieved everything you had ever dreamed of accomplishing in your career. In this moment of imagination you have the corporate title you most deserve. You have the salary, perks, authority and recognition befitting your talents and hard work. You've got a giant smile on your face as you think about all the people who benefit from the success you have earned. Your family is proud of you. Your colleagues come to you for advice and counsel. Even people outside your industry recognize you as one of the giants among corporate leaders.

Now, snap out of your imagination and grab hold of today's reality. You wouldn't be reading this book if you didn't see room for improvement. You want to hack the corporate ladder by getting all the secrets about how to do it from this book. You imagine this book can give you everything you've dreamed about in your career.

Here's the Bad News

Nothing and no one can make your rise through the corporate ladder easy. You will make mistakes. I know I have. You will also learn lessons as a result of those mistakes. It's all part of the process. You can, if you haven't already, let go of any notions of simply working hard, being recognized for your accomplishments and effortlessly rising to the top of the competitive corporate environment.

> "The great enemy of truth is very often not the lie – deliberate, contrived and dishonest – but the myth – persistent, persuasive and unrealistic."
> ~President Kennedy~

You are not that good. Truthfully – no one ever has been that good.

If you look around and see people who have seemingly succeeded because they were simply natural born leaders – you are not seeing the whole picture. Even people who enter the corporation with distinct advantages of being well connected to the higher echelons of the organization will fail if they depend totally on those advantages for their success. Corporations just don't work that way.

Promising Good News

This book is designed to give you "bread crumbs" on your path to hacking the corporate ladder successfully. Hopefully you will avoid some of the mistakes I made and you will embrace some of the wisdom found in this book. My goal is to make it much easier for you than it has been for me.

I am opening up the box where stories of success are hidden. This is not a motivational book with lots of encouragement and positive thinking. Instead, this is a pragmatic collection of actual stories from my own experience. In most cases the name of the person in the story has been changed. What's important for you to grasp is these stories represent real life in the corporate world.

Why Tell Stories?

Historians claim stories have been around for more than 27,000 years. When cave paintings were discovered it was

> *"Stories are how we learn best. We absorb numbers and facts and details, but we keep them all glued into our heads with stories"*
>
> ~Chris Brogan~

apparent many of them represented stories about life as a cave dweller. The reason why the earliest cave dwellers used stories etched into the walls of their surroundings is because they recognized stories are a powerful way to multiply the lesson beyond those you can communicate with directly with literal instruction. The cave wall stories helped anyone who happened to encounter the drawings.

There is a bigger reason at play too. Your brain is more likely to engage with a story than any lesson without one. A story goes beyond the language processing parts of your brain and activates the brain parts you would use if you were actually experiencing the story yourself. Truth is, evolution has hard wired our brains for storytelling.

I want you to get the most value out of this book possible. Although I hope you are entertained reading it, if all you get is entertainment I have failed in my own personal goals. What I hope for you is the lessons represented in these stories embed in your own psyche and guide you to your highest level of corporate success.

How the Book is Organized

Each section of the book is organized with both real-life stories about corporate life and a set of "Do's and Don'ts" you can use as a checklist in your corporate rise through the ranks. Although the book is a pretty good summary of my own experience, it does not claim to be the final word on success in corporate life. What I can assure you, if you follow the things told in this book you will rise through the ranks quicker and more easily than me. It is a handbook I would have loved to hold in my hands during the early years of my

> *"The delicate balance of mentoring someone is not creating them in your own image, but giving them the opportunity to create themselves"*
>
> ~Steven Spielberg~

career. I know I would have made fewer mistakes and learned the lessons much earlier in my career path.

Near the end of the book you will find my contact information. I would love to hear from you. It would help me to know what you enjoyed about the book and what stories you can tell about your own experience.

Expecting Your Success in
Hacking the Corporate Ladder!

1

EXPECT EXCELLENCE OF YOURSELF AND OTHERS

Excellence is a concept people tend to self-define. The word is often stated when referring to corporate expectations. Actually finding excellence in the workplace is a different thing all together.

Excellence is about our own personal brand and it is about the people-oriented and profit-maximizing practices within the entire organization. When you seek to hack the corporate ladder it is essential you align yourself with the principles of your company's definition of excellence. Furthermore, it pays to give close attention to the way you are perceived by others so you can maintain a reputation of excellence.

> "The magic formula that successful businesses have discovered is to treat customers like guests and employees like people."
> ~Tom Peters~

The book "In Search of Excellence" was a ground breaking study of 43 of America's best-run companies. The book was originally published in 1982. In 2012, Tom Peters reintroduced the book and made it a national #1 Best-Seller. Many leaders still consider this book essential to understanding corporate excellence.

Denise's Terrible Reputation

A young lady, Denise, came into my downline with a reputation for being obstinate and self centered. She had been perceived in this way for a long time. When a boss knows everything about you based on history, it can be very damaging.

I think she was a victim of poor management in the past and her experience caused her to give up. When I came into the organization to be her boss, I saw a spark of her in every wrong turn she took. We all take wrong turns from time to time. In her case she would get clobbered and people would say, *"There she goes again."* Others would just sit back and let these things happen to her. However, I can say I had noticed she had really turned things around.

> *"You can't build a reputation on what you are going to do."*
> ~Henry Ford~

Denise came into my office one day and said she really wanted to move to the next level. She was actually applying for a position with a peer of mine, but I knew this particular leader had a negative opinion of her based on her long standing reputation. I was very honest with her and brought up her bad reputation.

People had given up on her because she had given up. We sat down to look at the different areas where she actually showed improvement. She had a great story to tell, but had never told the story. So we worked through all of the story and I was able to endorse her.

> *"Your reputation is in the hands of others. That's what the reputation is. You can't control that. The only thing you can control is your character."*
> ~Wayne Dyer~

By taking the time to hear her story, I was able to both champion her with the peer leader and give her ammunition for her future conversation. I was fully aware if she were to simply apply for the position without a conversation, it was unlikely she would make it to the interview. The leader would likely play the old tapes and not given her consideration. Each of us must take responsibility for our actions and address them – particularly when we turn the corner.

My advice was for her to go to this other leader, share the story about how these issues have been corrected, and ask if he would consider her for the next move in her career. My peer came to me to ask my opinion. I shared my honest view of her improvement. She was given a chance and is now thriving in her new role. It was a real success story of damage control.

Portfolio of Work

A portfolio is your body of work you can show folks to demonstrate where you have made a difference. It doesn't matter how old you are or what position you are seeking, it is possible to create a portfolio of work.

There is a huge difference between a resume and a portfolio of your work. You can say whatever you want to say on your resume. People do it all the time. With a portfolio you can spell out your contribution and the specific good that came out of the work.

> *"Character comes from a Greek word meaning 'chisel' or 'the mark left by a chisel.' Of course, a chisel is a sharp steel tool used for making a sculpture out of a hard or difficult material, like granite or marble...You've got to chisel your character out of the raw material of yourself just like the sculptor has to create a statue."*
>
> ~Jim Rohn~

I recently worked with a college student. His name was Max and he didn't have any kind of a portfolio. He got turned down for a job where he applied and came back to me as his mentor. I asked about his portfolio and he felt he was too new to the work field to have built a portfolio.

We began building an action-based portfolio so he would have a nice document to go with his resume. It visually showed different contributions he had made in different jobs going all the way back to high school. The next time he interviewed he actually got the position. It's not the one thing that gets you the position, but it's a big part of it.

Customized Portfolio

In my current position, I was the obvious dark horse in the running. It was a high visibility

> *"Be a yardstick of quality. Some people aren't used to an environment where excellence is expected."*
>
> ~Steve Jobs~

job and a long interview process. I knew I needed to set myself apart. So I created a customized portfolio for each person interviewing me. In it I highlighted the work I knew they would be most interested in and how the work could contribute to the enterprise. As I went back into my body of work historically and told examples of project work I had executed, the interviewers were able to make a connection to the skills needed. This assured the interviewers that I had the skill set to be successful in the position and make the maximum contribution to the organization.

I find it is important that interviewers understand your work. There are plenty of examples I could share. For instance, if I'm talking about operational efficiency it may not push the same buttons for someone in human resources. A customized portfolio allows me to appeal to their "what's in it for me" need so they will give a thumbs up and offer their endorsement.

What I found out on the back side was I was the only candidate to have a portfolio. Since the others didn't have a portfolio it gave me an advantage. Again, it wasn't the single thing, but it was important.

Another time I interviewed for a position, I actually may have brought in too much of my project work. One thing I believe is too much is better than too little. When someone asks me if they should wear a tie to an interview, I tell them nobody's going to think ill of you if you wear a tie to an interview. Likewise, I rarely think you can bring too much portfolio work. If somebody has a question you'll be able to answer it and back it up.

The time I may have brought too much material I was interviewing with a director for a particular job. He looked at the volume of work and I don't know if he was impressed or overwhelmed. However, every question he asked me I was able to turn to it in my portfolio. He could see proof positive that I had the skill set to execute on the work they needed to be done in the particular position. I was offered the job and think everyone during that particular interview was happy I brought my portfolio of work.

So, I think for any position at any age a portfolio of work is relevant and an important differentiator.

Do's and Don'ts for Expecting Excellence

Do Trust

I start with trust because I believe it is important for you to trust people. It's commonly said people who don't trust are not trustworthy themselves. As we talk about this, my experience has been the old adage is true.

Do Verify

Coupled with trust, it's critical you verify. As leaders we're responsible for business and development of our people. It's important you verify because, as the leader, your name is on the bottom line. You want to trust, but you don't want to do it blindly. You want to verify it. Your leaders and employees will respect you for this and you won't get caught off guard.

Do Be Loyal

Loyalty is extremely important. I think loyalty is a sub category of good character. We can't always just sit on the fence. It doesn't mean you have to choose sides. But if you do choose sides, you have to be loyal. Folks do have memories. It's part of your character. If you pledge loyalty, you need to stay true to your word. Years ago when I was a lobbyist, my mentor Frank taught me "always dance with the one that brought you to the party".

Do Forgive

I have worked in some environments that are very, very unforgiving. Particularly when you look at organizations that have been around awhile and have longstanding employees of twenty plus years. You find someone might have a bad reputation because of something they did sixteen years ago.

If you hold a grudge against somebody you are unforgiving. It drives negativity around you damaging you as a leader and contributor to the organization. You might be overlooking a gem. Give people another chance. One of my CEO's used to say "that's why there are 3 strikes in baseball".

Do Believe

It's just one word, but I would say it encapsulates a lot. Believe in the good intent of others. Believe people are coming from the right place.

I think of a coworker of mine when I was around 25. He would often say, *"You probably think I hate everybody in the organization."* This individual had a problem with believing in people's good intent. I've noticed the individual is struggling in his career because he can't grasp this and experiences a lot of negativity.

There are very few people who come to work saying they want to sabotage the organization today. Most people come in with pride in their work. That's what we're talking about in the word "Believe."

Do Smile

Some of the things mentioned earlier like being positive, believing in people and inspiring don't happen if we don't smile. If we are grumpy all the time, it can undermine the building of other important qualities.

I think of a great boss who inspired me to great lengths. She had a terrible travel week before getting back to the office. The office was in bad condition and we were getting ready to close. We didn't realize it at the time. Anna came in and she was smiling. She was bright and inspiring to all of our people.

As her right hand person we met after the team meeting. She just about collapsed. She told me she felt terrible and she felt like crying but she couldn't let her people see her in a negative way. Anna was really fantastic and taught me a great lesson that day.

It's not about hiding how you feel. It's about giving your people, and those around you, what they need. It's giving them good energy.

Do Be Inspiring

Anyone who wants to move to the next level has to be inspirational. We don't want to follow people nor do we want to be led by people who can't inspire us. It's a really huge thing because if it's just managing work, anybody can do it. But not everybody can inspire. As a leader, coworker, individual contributor, you have the opportunity and responsibility to inspire. Sadly, many don't realize the value or responsibility of inspiring others.

~~~~ ~~~~ ~~~~ ~~~~ ~~~~ ~~~~ ~~~~ ~~~~ ~~~~

Don't Trash Others

There's no value in us as employees to knock down our peers or to run them into the ground. Most likely, if they aren't talented folks there's no reason for you to perpetuate the reputation. In the end, talent rises and sinks on its own.

Don't Talk Down to Folks

In this book I gave an example where I made this mistake. It was early in my career and I'd talk down to an employee. It was out of my own frustration, but it was damaging to the perception others had of me. We always want to be conscientious of recognizing people for their contribution. We have to be accountable but let's also celebrate all for their contribution.

Don't Be Afraid

In my own makeup I've had to work on this. As I have looked at individuals, at times I've lacked the courage to speak my mind with them. I will tell you the outcomes have always been greater when I was not afraid and had the courage to say or state what I believed.

I got some great advice from general counsel at a company. He told me I was hesitant when giving a negative feedback. He asked me for direct feedback and it was kind of negative. I was hesitant. Finally he looked at me and said, *"We don't pay you to do work. We pay you for your gray matter and your opinion. If you don't have the courage to give me your opinion I don't need to talk to you."* He wasn't being nasty but he needed some information. There was no vital wrong answer, but he needed an answer.

Don't Micromanage

If we start micromanaging folks we are telling them they don't know what they're doing. It also shows you don't trust they can do their work. If you do that, you're limiting your own bandwidth. You're damaging the relationship with the individual and it's not adding any value. You won't micromanage if you trust and verify instead.

Don't Pressure Folks

Be open to the opinion of others. Not everybody has the same opinion so pressure tends to really bring a negative environment around us. Let people bring their contribution as they can. Be encouraging and supportive but don't pressure. Pressure breeds unhealthy behaviors and creates toxic environments. Don't confuse this with holding people accountable.

ROBERT T. GOFOURTH

2

BE AUTHENTICALLY HUMAN… FAULTS & ALL

In 2005, the Harvard Business Review published a five year study defining authenticity. In the publication they describe the benefits and qualities of authenticity in leadership. They quickly admit almost everyone misunderstands authenticity. Leaders even misunderstand what is expected by the term.

The article points out, "No leader can look into a mirror and say, "I am authentic." A person cannot be authentic on his or her own. Authenticity is largely defined by what other people see in you...In fact, authenticity is a quality that others must attribute to you."

The study boiled the authenticity challenge into two parts:
1. The leader must ensure their words are consistent with their deeds. Without this level of consistency, followers will never accept you as authentic. People instinctively recognize fraudulent behavior. A great leader is at least a little obsessive about living authentically – day in and day out.

2. Finding common ground with the people you lead (and follow) is the second challenge. This means an authentic leader presents different aspects of yourself to different audiences. Although they may show a different part of themselves to the CEO than to a new hire, they never fall into fake leadership with leader-like sound bites of things leaders might say.

Authentic leaders are comfortable in their own skin when they are speaking to their superiors or downline. They know being a leader is more complicated than simply behaving like a leader. When they approach their colleagues in an authentic way, it gives followers self-respect and value. An ability to be true to self changes the attitude of everyone around them. Performance and product quality improve.

Part of being authentic is being vulnerable, human and making mistakes. While some may focus on the need to be confident and competent, we know a good leader also possesses qualities of humility. Being able to admit mistakes and accept help from others is a powerful way to lead. We have all had the experience of "being in way over our head" and a good leader is willing to be gracious in such situations. They put their own ego aside to embrace what is good for the organization.

Vulnerability is the birthplace of innovation, creativity and change."

~ Dr Brene Brown ~

Leaders also assume risk when they avoid being a dictator. Rather than exerting their will over others, they leave room for others to act. As the person ultimately responsible for outcomes, they are exposed to potential criticism or pushback from others. They are charged with identifying and rectifying mistakes...while fully understanding authenticity and mistakes are a part of every life.

What I Learned From Angela

Oftentimes folks really feel people view them the way they view themselves. I have learned the hard way this is not true. I've made some mistakes. Some of my mistakes have hung with me over the years. I love to tell stories on myself because we can learn from ourselves and the stories are very advantageous. Here's a story about one of those mistakes.

I was working for a financial services organization and the company was closing down operations on the East Coast. I had a very close working relationship with my counterpart, Jackie, on the West Coast. She asked me "Please don't just send me a bunch of sloppy work to finish up."

This was many years ago and we didn't have electronic files like today. Paper files were how we managed everything.

"When we were children, we used to think that when were grown-up we would no longer be vulnerable. But to grow up is to accept vulnerability...To be alive is to be vulnerable."

~ Madeleine L'Engle ~

I didn't really know anything about different communication styles and people having different personalities. I now know those differences all add to the fabric of an organization.

Angela was one of my employees. She was a social butterfly and was going around saying bye to people. People were her motivation.

Whereas I really like to get the work out. So I went to her desk, grabbed her files and rather rudely belted out across the office asking if anyone wants to do some work here today. It was clear to me Angela doesn't want to do her work.

The next thing I knew Angela was there crying in her office about what I said saying she didn't want to do her work. It made me realize if I ever worked with Angela again the relationship was damaged. While Angela and I haven't worked together since, I have worked with people who witnessed that action.

So, it was important for me to go back and solicit what their opinion was of me later. Even though years had passed, I knew I might have to do some mending because I looked like an uncaring leader. I was trying to do something good for the company and our coworkers on the West Coast and simply made a mistake.

If I had it to do over again, I'd go to Angela and say, "Hey, these people on the West Coast are going to be killed by all this work." Telling Angela about other people would have struck a chord with her. But I didn't know that then.

No matter how little the offense might be, you need to go back and talk to folks. Learn how they feel about you because you may need to course correct something and fix something from the past.

My Lesson From Jeremy

I had another employee named Jeremy. He was extremely good at his job. He was a young manager. I had not yet learned to solicit opinions of folks who reported to me. It was something I figured out with Jeremy.

We were at dinner and during a casual conversation, he let me know how I deeply offended him and hurt his feelings. In reality I was trying to give him some coaching notes about his personal appearance. I wanted him to ramp up his personal appearance. But he felt more like I had attacked him.

Sitting down and listening to Jeremy in this casual environment allowed him to be very honest with me. It let me know he had probably a different opinion of the situation than I did.

We are all faced with these sort of things just because we are human. Again, it's really important to solicit information from people. You want to know how they view you and what they remember about the situation. It allows us to know when to course correct.

Damage Control - Getting Over the Past

"Trust is the glue of life. It's the most essential ingredient in effective communication. It's the foundational principle that holds all relationships."

~ Stephen R. Covey ~

Damage control is when your reputation has been tarnished or influenced by your actions. The opinion of others may have been influenced by actions you directly or indirectly participated in yourself. It can be gossip. It can be sloppy work. It can be your own interactions with others. It could even be the attitude you bring toward interpersonal relationship.

It can take a multitude of different forms. You really just need to look at any situation by going back and asking how people view you. If there is any damage to the way people perceive you, you must go back and rework the perception so people know who you really are.

Where I work today, people have a lot of longevity. Finding someone who's been in place over twenty years is commonplace. Something I have found in these situations is you could have stubbed your toe sixteen years ago and someone's going to remember it, right? So if you haven't gone back and corrected damage, wherever the damage exists, it is vitally important to take action on damage control.

Oftentimes I have been off base on what I think people interpret. This is a situation where I would really encourage everybody to agree to round the table to their leaders, to the people that report to them and to their peer group. It allows us to get a 360 degree view of how people perceive us. It's critical.

My Boss Rick

My relationship with Rick began when I had to make a very unpopular recommendation to eliminate positions in one area of the business. Rick was the leader of this particular business unit and he was extremely displeased with my assessment of the situation. He was extremely resistant. In fact the issue escalated to the level of the president CEO of the division. Our boss decided to support my recommendation and the positions were eliminated. Rick was not happy with me at all.

No one likes this sort of difficult negotiations between coworkers. It didn't matter because I was doing the right thing for the company. While Rick and I got along fine, there was always a little something there between us.

My personal challenge came when the president of the division left and Rick became the new president. Overnight he became my new boss. We had a little history so I knew I had to go back to Rick and explain why we made those decisions. I wanted him to see the decision was good for the enterprise.

Once we were able to do that he understood the decision was the right thing for the business. He now could look from the perspective of the entire enterprise, rather than only seeing the situation from the regional level.

"Conviction, commitment, credibility; the three pillars of morally courageous leadership."

~ General John Michel ~

Going back and doing damage control was important for us. Even though it was the right thing for the business, it still could have had a negative outcome on me. Over the time we worked together I became a trusted advisor to him and we had a very strong work relationship. He encouraged me to take on a global role and become an expat working on a challenging account. Rick knew the value I could bring and became a huge supporter for me and did a lot for my career.

Lessons on Damage Control from Wayne

Early in my career, when I was in my mid-twenties, I thought I knew everything...as many twenty-something folks do. Martha, an office manager in second command and I had a difference of opinion. I can't tell you exactly what got us sideways, but when she worked to get my work area next to her, I immediately had an attitude. I took severe issue with this and immediately knew I could show them the error of their way by being obstinate.

I quickly flew into a nosedive. During this uncomfortable situation I didn't even think of all the damage I was creating. People were watching me and how I was reacting. My attitude and performance quickly was out of sorts and it was noticed by our mutual boss Wayne. Even though I was in my mid-twenties and already had a good reputation for the business, this bad attitude damaged the way people thought about me.

Eventually Wayne called me into his office to share a similar story about himself. He pointed out that when it seems like the problem is everybody else it's time to look in the mirror.

> "A man must be big enough to admit his mistakes, smart enough to profit from them, and strong enough to correct them."
>
> ~ John Maxwell ~

The following week I went into Wayne's office and thanked him. I knew I was wrong and I also knew I needed to correct his opinion of me. A few months later Wayne asked me to move a few hours north to open the new regional office. If Wayne had not seen my growth and ability to shore up my shortcomings, he would not have entrusted me with the new position. While long since retired, Wayne is still a mentor to me today.

It's something I really try to do each time there is a challenge. When business becomes hard, whether inside or outside the office, we need to take a look in the mirror. We need to look for the damage created. We need to determine our own part in the damage and course correct.

It's been my experience when folks are unwilling to identify their own role in the problem they continually have a bad reputation. They don't care about the damage created.

I have someone who I consider a close friend. He finds himself continually struggling to get to the next level. It's because she refuses to go back and look at the damage so she can course correct. Even though words may not be spoken, folks are watching. It is critical we look at damage control.

Damage can happen to us early on and have devastating effects if we allow it to remain. Even if it seems like you are in the right – or it won't have an impact – always ask what your part is in the situation and take corrective action.

Boss with All the Answers

Ryan was a really good guy. He was extremely intelligent but his unwillingness to be vulnerable really hurt him. I found while working with him, and a consistent client base over the years, his confident answers for clients caused people to not trust him. In the end, he didn't come off as authentic. People seemed to know.

> *"The things worth learning are the things you learn after you know it all."*
>
> ~ Harry S. Truman ~

According to Ryan, he had no weaknesses. I was having a private dinner with one of our biggest clients one evening and as we talked she remarked, *"Ryan is full of B.S. You know, he never admits when your company can't do something. You guys are very good at what you do. But he acts like you have all the answers and no one person has all of the answers."*

She went on to say she would continue to buy services from us in the future, but she had developed a distrust. She felt forced to engage in deeper due diligence because she didn't know if we could perform the work because of Ryan having all the "answers."

Ryan had created trust issues around this individual. Therefore, although the client loved us, there wasn't any way she could automatically move us to the next level through trust. Because Ryan was not authentic and vulnerable, it created a trust barrier. He actually made our selling cycle more difficult – at least with this particular client. We only talked about our strengths to the point we never admitted any weakness…and drove the perception of lacking authenticity.

It is no different in any relationship – professional or personal. Individuals like to see you are like them. They want to see you have an opportunity to grow as well. If you are not authentic and show people your gaps on occasion, they will not trust to move you to the next level with them.

In fact, I remember interviewing a job candidate. When we started talking about gaps and weaknesses, the lady said, *"Well, I don't have any gaps."* In my mind the interview was immediately over because she was telling me she didn't have an opportunity to grow. All of the sudden I decided if she can't grow, she probably can't go to the next level because she's stuck. Based on my experience, I made a good decision about her.

I Don't Know the Answer

There have been a number of occasions when people ask me a question. If I don't know, I will flat out tell them I don't know the answer.

In my most current position we encounter many unknown answers to many questions around the industry and we have

> *"I think on some level, you do your best things when you're a little off-balance, a little scared. You've got to work from mystery, from wonder, from not knowing."*
>
> ~ Willem Dafoe~

a few internal issues too. I have a lunch meeting with my employees once a month. It is voluntary and very casual. There have been a number of occasions when an employee will ask a question and I simply don't know the answer.

I remember a particular employee, her name was Sally. She asked a question in a meeting. I said I don't know the answer. I'll do my best to find out and will let you know. Later she came to me and told me she had come from a larger corporation. She shared that my counterpart at that company would have never said *"I don't know."* She complimented me on the way I handled things and remarked, *"Your brand of leadership is so refreshing. It's so authentic and I know I can trust you."*

Authenticity is a foundation of leadership that will propel you to the next level. When you look at those you will lead, they must be able to trust you. If they don't trust you, and your brand will be damaged. Your employees have the ability to make or break your reputation. Without sincere authenticity, this one thing will impede you from getting to the next level.

I know I have said it a couple of times, but the kind of 360 degree view of people's opinions is critical to climbing the corporate ladder. Talk about your strengths as well as weaknesses – because in our weaknesses we build strengths. We already have our strengths. It is the weaknesses that add us to the next level.

Do's and Don'ts About Authenticity

Do Be Yourself

I'm going to start with a political comparison as a side note. I think it is a very easy example to understand. When I was speaking at a university shortly after the first Obama election, one of the young ladies in the audience asked for my advice to young women going into business. Immediately, the idea of being yourself popped into my mind.

I used an example of the prior first lady, Hillary Clinton compared to Michelle Obama. When we look at the two personalities you see that one really embraces herself. The other embraces the personality of what society thinks she should be. I think one feels authentic and one does not.

I use the word authentic. We talk about some examples in this book to show how much I think authenticity is so important. If the people you work with do not believe you are authentic you lose your ability to lead, people's trust breaks down and they start questioning your motives.

Do Know Who You Are

Take your inventory and know what makes you up as a person. Know your attributes and know your deficits. Work on both of them. You want to make your strengths stronger. You probably want to work first on your weaknesses so we can really build a stronger individual.

Once you start the self realization process, it's easier to do some of the things we've talked about like being authentic and being more humble because you know what makes you up as a person.

Do Be Unusual

I had a much older mentor by the name of Frank during one of my jobs. I was a lobbyist for a couple of years and he told me, *"You have to be unusual."* You have to have something that sets you apart. It really doesn't matter what it is. It doesn't matter if it's a catchphrase. It doesn't matter if you wear a bow tie every day or wear cuff links every day. My first corporate boss, Wayne, wore cufflinks every single day of his life. It was something very unusual, but it was definitely his signature.

What's important is there needs to be something unusual people associate with you and your brand. It kind of keeps you top of mind when you're working with other people trying to get to the next level. It doesn't mean weird and quirky. It's something you give yourself as a signature setting yourself apart from everybody else. By the way, I wear cufflinks every day!

Do Be Connected with All

One of my favorite books is "*Lincoln on Leadership*." In it they talk about how Lincoln would move along the troops. He would go out amongst them and be connected with folks. You know the connection is important because it lets you know what's on people's minds. It lets you really hold tight to their condition and let them know you care. It's part of authenticity. Connection is important. I remember one young lady who was in my reporting line. In one of my frequent walk arounds, I introduced myself to her and asked her what she did at the company. She said "oh, I don't do anything important, I just open the mail". I realized at this moment that as a company, we had diminished this individual's contribution. I explained to her that not one contract could be underwritten without her opening that piece of mail. Not one policy could be effectuated without her opening that premium check. Without hearing what is on our employees minds, we really don't know what is going on in the organization.

Do Be Caring

We have endured many years of aggressive leaders in business. However, I think if people know you genuinely care about them, they will support you in your endeavor to move up the ladder. They will want to work for you. Being caring doesn't mean you don't hold people accountable. Being caring really means you care about them as people, their contribution and the alignment.

Recently one of my employees had to shuffle people around because they didn't have the right skill set to do the job. She is displaying care for those people by putting them in a position where they can contribute the most and can succeed instead of fail.

So care doesn't always feel warm and fuzzy. But care is multifaceted. We have to look at what's behind the care and motivation. I would say I could have been more aware of this early on in my career. I could have noticed some things about the motives of people around me. I made some mistakes because I wasn't aware of different movement around me and it was detrimental to my career. I would say I even had situations where people didn't have the best intent. Because I wasn't aware, and a little naïve even, there was a negative outcome for me.

Do Have Passion

Of course, most of us work because we have to work. We have to earn a living. But boy, it makes a big difference when we can get in to a job fitting where we have passion around what we do. If you don't have passion it affects your contribution and people around you will notice whether you are leading your peer group or being noticed by the people you report to. If you don't have passion for your work, my recommendation would be to find a position you do have passion around. You won't make it to the next level if you don't have passion.

Do Have Vision

Along with passion you have to have vision. If everybody else sits beside you and contributes at the same level you're not different. Anybody can give you that level of contribution. If you have vision, you can couple it with what makes you different to get a different type of highly valuable contribution to offer the organization.

Do Be Present

We are all distracted by our smart phones and email, even when we are sitting at our desk. I have been very guilty of not being present in the past when in a meeting. If you're not connected with the person you are in the meeting with, it undermines the other things in this list. A lot of the things on this list feed off each other and are connected in some way. Be present, be connected.

Do Be Generous

I think we have to have a heart for people. We have to understand where they're coming from. Again it doesn't mean we don't hold folks accountable. I think being generous in our understanding and caring for our coworkers can really excel you to the next level. I believe leaders possess the quality of being generous in many different ways.

Do Be Highly Ethical and of Good Character

It's easy for us to point to leaders in the past who have been fine leaders but they have not necessarily been of good character. When this happens their ability to influence coworkers and peers is damaged. It has impaired their ability to lead. I never ever forget character is something you own. It's something you have to build and invest in. If you lose it, it takes a lifetime to rebuild it.

~~~ ~~~ ~~~ ~~~ ~~~ ~~~ ~~~ ~~~ ~~~ ~~~

Don't Get Disappointed or Hurt

If someone doesn't approach you about a job to take you to the next level, or you are not selected for a position, don't get disappointed. Your disappointment talks to your make up and your chance will come if you follow these formulas. If people see you are hurt by the situation, it will hurt your brand overall.

Don't Think Everyone is Your Friend

I think of examples of folks who have told me they're my good friend. You know, in business it is very nice to have friendly relationships at work. However, most likely we are here at any company because we need to earn a living. Hopefully it's something we enjoy and hopefully we like the people who work with us. You may become friends with somebody, but to go out and declare everybody as your friend is not a good idea. Doing it will speak to your confidence and it can speak to your judgment. Not everybody will have the same opinion of the person. If you appear to be highly aligned with someone it can be detrimental. So I always caution people on using the friend word.

Don't Get Wild

When I was interviewing for a corporate officer position, the C.O.O. told me if I was to get hired for the position, I would be a fiduciary of the company. He explained we all like to have a good time, but don't be wild. He explained that I would always be known as an officer of the company, not just as employee. Be of good humor and all that, but we always want to be responsible.

3

Networking and Self Promotion

It's not likely you will land the job you want to move up in your career while sitting behind your computer submitting online applications. The business world has always been a "who you know" environment and nothing is going to change the reality.

LinkedIn did a [joint study](#) asking people how they found their most recent job. With about 3,000 people reporting, the data indicates up to 85% of all jobs are filled by some type of networking connection. Networking gives you "back door" access to a hidden job market of unadvertised positions.

Networking is not about asking for a job. Use your networking conversations to develop meaningful relationships and it may lead to an incredible opportunity. Don't focus on large numbers of contacts. Be selective when growing your network.

> "Never lose sight of the fact that the most important yardstick of your success will be how you treat other people – your family, friends and coworkers, and even strangers you meet along the way."
>
> ~ Barbara Bush ~

There is nothing wrong with having thousands of contacts in your social media, but you cannot maintain more than about 150 meaningful relationships. When you are choosing how to spend your networking time you want to focus on those who have the potential of a genuinely social relationship.

Networking is important outside your current company, but it is equally important to network inside your current company. Talk to people in other areas of the enterprise and interact with them enough to learn what is required for success in their areas. The more you know about how other areas of the company operate, the more effective you can be in your current position. Also, showing interest in the work of others makes you more likely to be considered for a new, more challenging position.

Story About My Twin Brother

My brother wanted to advance in his company for quite a while. I've known Randy, one of the company's senior vice presidents, for about twenty-five years. In one of our brotherly conversations my brother says "Randy knows who I am and he has a high opinion of me. He wants me to move forward."

I asked my brother how Randy knew he wanted the position and he said, "Oh, we had lunch a few years ago and I told him then." I tried to explain that a lot of water had passed under the bridge in the past few years. With tens of thousands of employees in the organization, my brother needed to go back to touch base. He needed to step up and make sure Randy knows he wants to move forward and have Randy's endorsement.

Networking Inside the Organization

Extracurricular activities at your company can be highly valuable to your efforts to move up the corporate ladder.

Although these activities are generally optional, I have found them to be extremely important to my career.

- The activities allow you to develop a deeper relationship with those on an equal or lower status in the company while outside the office. The activity "humanizes" you in a way not accomplished in the average business day.

- You are able to connect on a personal level with people in a higher position than yourself. While you may go into the activity with a reasonably good relationship, spending time getting to know people on a higher level opens doors to reaching out to them later.

Senior Vice President Bob

It never intimidated me to interact with higher level executives in or out of the office. Good relationships are strengthened in the personal interactions of extracurricular activities when they are handled in an appropriate way. In one of my previous positions, I had the

> *"The richest people in the world look for and build networks, everyone else looks for work."*
>
> ~ Robert Kiyosaki ~

occasion to go to our home office in Minneapolis often. We would always do something fun.

Bob, one of the senior vice presidents often sponsored something like a bowling or baseball game or as a volunteer at charity events. I would go for more than simply enjoying myself. I recognized the value in the opportunity to get to know Bob on a personal level. It was hard to spend much time with him in the office. With the informal relationship he was able to see the value I brought to the table, and what he wanted from me, while we interacted in a very casual way.

I have been downsized a few times and this was another situation where my position was eliminated. I was able to pick up the phone and call Bob and say *"Hey, if you hear of any jobs, just let me know."* This was a day when thousands of people had been let go. Later that week Bob called me up and said *"Yeah, I've got a buddy in Detroit and he saw the newspaper article that we let a lot of people go. If you want me to pass your name and number on to him I will."*

The next week I actually had an interview with the company and got the job. If I had not made the effort to develop a personal relationship with Bob, built on a casual kind of networking extracurricular activity, I probably wouldn't have the comfort level to just call him up and say if you hear of something let me know. As well, I was far enough removed from him in the company that he would not have known me or had a comfort level in recommending me to his colleague.

For me, the one thing I found to be very important was the internal networking at outside events. I really enjoyed having fun with my company colleagues. While extracurricular activities feel simply "fun" in nature, it pays to search for the underlying value in them. It actually paid off for me and my future career. It's an excellent story of how well the networking can work for you.

Networking Outside the Organization

Activities with people outside the office is also critically important. During one of the several downsizings I experienced in my career, I was volunteering at a charitable event. I met Steve. As we got to talking, I told Steve I had just been laid off. As luck would have it, Steve's sister was a senior executive with a global leader in health and beauty.

He introduced me to his sister the next week. The following week I was sitting on the 41st floor of their World Headquarters on 5th Avenue in Manhattan. My buddy who's in the industry was floored that I had the interview.

In the end I did not get the position because I simply did not have the industry experience. However, I did get the interview for what could have been the next level of my career. When you infuse the right amount of professionalism and career objective you never know who you're going to meet while you are having some cookies and punch at a holiday party.

Through networking outside the office you will make connections. You never know where those connections will lead. The fact is, just because the person you are talking to doesn't have the position you want, it doesn't mean they don't know someone who has the position you want.

Seek Mentor Connections

Important connections can come from the most unusual places.

> *"If you want to go fast, go alone. If you want to go far, go with others."*
>
> ~ African Proverb ~

Once, when I was already in an executive position, my CEO wanted to create an enterprise risk management discipline. First, I didn't know anything about enterprise risk management. Second, this was pretty much a lateral move as a peer to my current position.

I knew it would add to my skill set, I would earn more money and assist me in getting to the next level. I decided to go to the local association and ask for contact information for local enterprise risk management professionals. The referrals led me to John who spent an inordinate number of hours over several months preparing me to have a strong foundation in risk management. I interviewed for the job and was ultimately selected.

What I didn't know about John when we began working together is he is a world renowned risk manager and served as president of the Risk and Insurance Management Society. He volunteered a lot of time to help me learn about enterprise risk. He is dedicated to the profession and admired the fact I was willing to learn a new discipline. John is someone I continually look to for professional advice. I have continued to collaborate with John to this day.

I think taking the initiative to seek out an individual who is really good in the industry specific to your business is a good idea. Look for an expert who was in the job you want. The fact is people enjoy sharing their knowledge…particularly when someone has a desire to learn and spread the discipline. Spend the time to partner with them. Understand where they're coming from and take full advantage of their knowledge. Finding someone with the skill set I needed to do a new job let me learn the tactical and strategic approaches around the position I wanted.

Formal Coaching

Using a coach from outside the company can make a huge difference. They have no ties to politics, old tapes around your skill set or internal interactions. Instead, they know how to benchmark you against potential competitors and up-market you. For the most part, they are not biased and can give you solid guidance.

At one point in my career I was fairly new to my position but I knew I wanted to move to the next level. I knew it was time for me to contribute at my top level for the company. I worked with Trudy, a fairly aggressive coach who told me I had a strong skill set and I would move on from the current position fairly quickly.

This coach is hard hitting and doesn't take any prisoners. She quickly gave me coaching notes around my strengths and weaknesses. She understood where I wanted to end up and when she believed I was ready she pushed me hard. Trudy's approach has helped many leaders, including me, to the next level.

In my current position, Trudy is somebody who I've relied on to say what I need to do and points out my weaknesses. Working with a strong coach like Trudy forces you to have an open mind to listen and take the hard feedback. When they help you identify those gaps you must act on them. You want someone who will shoot straight with you.

In full transparency, Trudy is paid a fair sum of money to give this sort of advice. You don't want to work with somebody who's going to stroke your ego and make you feel good about what you do. You should get the positive feedback during your annual review of your accomplishments. When you're really looking to move to the next level you want to understand your opportunities to improve. You want to act on those opportunities so you can become better.

Guidance from a formalized coaching relationship can be expensive. However, a good coach does not need to be compensated. You simply need somebody who's going to be honest with you and help you grow.

Collaborate with Truth Tellers

As a younger manager I was resistant to those who were willing to acknowledge my weaknesses. I learned quickly of the benefits of partnering with somebody I wanted to be like and would be honest about my weaknesses.

> *"In a time of universal deceit, telling the truth is a revolutionary act."*
>
> ~ George Orwell ~

I think of a long time buddy of mine named Murphy. We've been friends for a long, long time. We've partnered on projects through the years. I will say he embodies the achievement I want for my own life.

Today Murphy is a CEO of a global company. He's had great achievements. I recognized he was somebody I looked up to and liked. He knows my objective but also has the ability to spot what is needed to move to the next level.

Early in my career most of my positions were obtained through networking and an offer normally came. I wanted a new position and had to actually apply and interview for it. After the interview, I went to my friend Murphy and shared my answers to some of the interview questions. He pointed out where I had provided less than optimal answers. I did not get the job. As I reviewed my answers he was quickly able to say, you know what, this is where you missed it. In retrospect it would have been much better for me to partner with this person I respect before the interview instead of after the interview.

To this day I don't make a move without collaborating with Murphy.

Individuals who really know you are able to clearly tell you your gaps. As long as the person you admire is totally honest with you and give you feedback, you can start emulating some of the things they do. Working with this information you can shore up the identified weaknesses. Coupled with your goals, this collaboration can be extremely valuable in getting you to the next level.

Do's and Don'ts About Networking

Do Watch for Opportunity

In some parts of my career, particularly with becoming an expat, I could have been in a really bad situation if I had not made a move. I had the chance to change my career and learned about watching for opportunity. You have to jump when you see the opportunities show up.

You need faith to drive you to overcome fear. By watching for opportunity you create a different person for yourself within business. Within the organization, taking advantage of these opportunities can be a big differentiator between you and everybody else.

Do Know Why You Want to Advance

Here I am at forty eight and obviously not as young as I used to be. More and more young people come to me (honestly they're not all young) and they say they want to move to the next level. I am surprised by their answer when I ask why they want to move up.

Some will say they want this title or more money. If that's your motivation, it's probably going to create additional challenges for you. Really, if you want to advance, it needs to be around contribution and making the organization better. It has to be more selfless.

I would also say if someone doesn't possess this view…if their motivation to move up is title or money driven, you will know it's not time to take the next move. Because if you take the next move and those are your motivators, you will most likely not succeed. You will not necessarily be happy. We all know money makes somebody happy on the first pay cycle. After that, it's not a motivator anymore because we already have it.

Do Partner with Others

We've talked about skill set and knowing who we are and it is important to have partners. As we network inside companies, our industry, and outside in the community you want partners for collaboration. I think of a high performing team I used to work with previously. All of us have moved on to great levels in our career. One of the things we hung to during our time together is - one and one isn't two, on this team, one and one is three. It's through collaboration and partnership we all found greater success.

Do Network Smartly

Clearly understand the value of networking. It's more than going out to have a drink and some appetizers. Networking needs to be purposeful. You want to learn what you can contribute to the other individual and what they can contribute to you. Exchange ideas and really learn about the person you are meeting. It is much more than simply an activity. A networking meeting needs a purpose.

Do Self Promote

Many people will say you are self centered when you self promote. I will tell you if you do not speak of yourself as an authority, as the best person for the job, nobody else is going to do it for you. Self promotion is not a set of dirty words. It is something we all have to do. You have to believe in yourself.

I think of a fellow I interviewed and remember the precise

moment I was done with the interview. He said, *"I rarely hit a home run but I always make it to base."* My mental response was, *"OK great, so you're average."*

It might sound a little cold hearted but you can't be on my team if you're average. Right? So, I look for talent.

Now I know this individual and he's a great contributor. But when he told me that I started questioning his belief in his own ability to contribute. So, self promotion is not a bad thing at all.

Do Know Who You are Hitched to

In my career I have often gotten advice saying I needed to forge a relationship with a particular individual. They said if I didn't do this I would not succeed in the organization. Most recently, the person I was trying to forge a relationship and align with left the company. With this departure, all of my investment in them was gone.

The good news is I hitched myself to a few different people. I didn't put all my eggs in one basket. You really want to understand who you are aligning with.

~~~~ ~~~~ ~~~~ ~~~~ ~~~~ ~~~~ ~~~~ ~~~~ ~~~~

Don't Oversell or Over Close

I remember times in my past where I have seen people who tend to oversell or over close on an idea. It can happen when they are trying to sell themselves as employees on an interview. It shows lack of confidence. Once you have the connection, just go ahead and move on to recognize those signs.

Don't Treat People Differently

It's a cold hard fact there are people we like better than others. But when we're working with folks we can't treat them differently. You know we need to apply the ruler to everybody equally – whether it's positive or negative.

Don't Be Intimidating

I've had some bosses in the past who were intimidating. When the boss is intimidating it takes away from the success of the environment around you. If the environment starts to fail or it just starts a vacuum where folks don't think they are a fit to go to the next level, you can create talent flight risks that end up weakening the organization.

Don't Be Fake

The fact is, people know if you're sincere. People know when you're authentic. When you are fake it can really damage your brand. It gets back to the importance of embracing authenticity and honesty. There is no reason to be fake. We find sometimes people are fake because they lack the courage to be honest or in some cases, covering up incompetence.

4

NEVER LOSE SIGHT OF YOUR PRIORITIES

Life is busy. Business is busy. Your role in your company is busy.

Sometimes all the "busy-ness" can distract us from our highest priorities. Few things can sabotage our rise up the corporate ladder more than losing sight of what is important – to ourselves, those we love and the priorities of the organization where we work.

We wear a lot of hats and deal with a constant barrage of issues. If we don't focus on our priorities, each day's tasks can become a jumbled mess shifting from one emergency to the next.

> *"Every well-built house started with a definite plan in the form of blueprints."*
>
> ~ Napoleon Hill ~

While sometimes a day can be filled with low-level priorities, it is critical you have a solid "big picture" in mind. The overarching philosophy will serve as a foundation for the daily decisions. Without the strict adherence to your most important priorities, your entire strategy for climbing the corporate ladder will run the risk of falling apart.

Executive Decisions

When you are responsible for leading others, your personal vision becomes even more essential. You must be creative and constructive. You must navigate the complex culture of the organization and keep your eye on profitability. With your priorities firmly in place, you can trust your instincts and lead your downline.

No matter how gifted you may be, you have to remember no one succeeds alone. Fostering a "we" mindset will take you much further in the organization than the "me" mindset with a focus on yourself. Build a diverse team. Cultivate a sense of adventure about your work. Pay attention to the small details without losing sight of the big goals.

The Catch-22 of Experience

We hear the question, "How do you get experience if people will only hire those with experience." In the urban dictionary, a Catch-22 is defined as, "A requirement that cannot be met until a prerequisite requirement is met, however, the prerequisite cannot be obtained until the original requirement is met." Sounds pretty impossible doesn't it.

In my career I have twice come into companies at a lower level than I felt I was qualified. In both instances, I was promoted in a very short amount of time.

Now we all know if you are severely overqualified for a job, you may not get hired. But if the offering is one level below your qualifications, my recommendation would be to go ahead and accept the lower level position. A lot of times our opinion is we think we are higher on the ladder than we really are. Going in at the lower perceived level allows you to start showing folks your skill and contribution. When others see what you can bring to the table you will be promoted quickly.

This has worked for me. At Citizen Property Insurance I was brought in as Director of Continuous Quality Improvement. During that period, I just brought my value to the table. I showed the skills needed to lead. During my time as Director of CQI, I focused on quickly adding value to the organization and finding wins.

When an opening for Vice President of Operations presented itself, Scott the CEO came to me. He acknowledged my contribution. He said he recognized my talent and skill set. He asked me to apply for the opening as VP of Operations. I applied, interviewed and was promoted to the position. This all happened within less than a year of coming to the company.

My willingness to come in at a lower level at Citizens enabled me to move up quickly. Often there is only a window for you to enter into the right organization. If you become great at your job in short order, and add value to the organization, you will be recognized when other opportunities present themselves.

It would have been great to have been hired into the position. Initially I wasn't viewed as having the skill set. So I was willing to go in there and showed them what I could do. Maybe someone thought I didn't have the right experience, but once I was able to demonstrate in a working situation, they saw I definitely had the experience needed for the position.

So often people will not consider signing on because they get hung up on titles and position. In reality they should focus on the work and the contribution. The next level will present itself.

Internships, Volunteering and Shadowing

"Consistently applied forward movement – not thought, not spirit, not attitude – is the most important factor in success. Today is the best day in your life to get moving."

~ Michael Masterson ~

Younger people have several ways to get experience before they are hired for the first official, paying job. Even someone more set in their career will benefit from working in a non-paid position. It could be work around being a volunteer in an organization, shadowing or internships.

There was a young man by the name of Dennis. He needed a summer internship. He went to the organization where he wanted to work after graduation. The executive director interviewed him and told him they don't hire anyone without nonprofit experience.

Although he didn't land an internship at his first choice company, the interview was extremely valuable to Dennis. He recognized if he wanted to work for this particular company, he must have nonprofit experience. I was able to connect him with a different, smaller nonprofit. He gained the nonprofit experience he needed. After college he was able to go to the organization and find a position. Being qualified educationally would not have landed him the job without the nonprofit experience.

Some students gain benefit from job shadowing. In other words, while it is an unpaid position similar to an internship, it normally is only one day of walking through a work day with a competent worker. It is a popular way to get some on-the-job learning and workplace exposure as part of career development.

All of these are ways to come into an organization to get experience. These activities can start to give you credence and skills when you don't necessarily have the formal experience.

Performance and Annual Reviews

If you have a leader who gives honest performance reviews, it can be a great starting point for closing your gaps. You want to be told your strengths and your opportunities to improve. You can then focus on the weaker areas and become better. It is something I've done in my career in an effort to close the gaps in my interactions or whatever exercise might be needed.

"Three Rules of Work:

Out of clutter find simplicity; from discord find harmony; in the middle of difficulty lies opportunity."

~ Albert Einstein ~

I've gone back to my boss and told her I have worked on this and just wanted to let you know. When I do this, my boss sees I take the feedback seriously. They are aware I am working on closing the gaps pointed out in the review. Also, when the time is right for me to move to the next level, she won't need to worry about me closing the gaps. The boss is confident I've addressed them along the journey. She knows I am ready for the next level.

A valuable tool for climbing the corporate ladder is your connection with the current organization. The past performance review is really important. If you don't have midpoint assessments, you should check in with your boss to tell them of the work you are doing to close the gaps. It shows you are being proactive. When you are proactive rather than reactive it shows you are ready for the next level of leadership. It also shows that you are taking a strategic view of your career rather than a tactical view.

Dissect Your Resume

I recently hired an individual who I knew was very, very talented. However, as we looked at her current job title, it did not reflect her ability to be qualified for the position. Her previous job titles did not align with the work needed. We knew the skills set and experience was there, but it was not obvious from her resume.

I would encourage anyone to dig into your resume and uncover your work history. Understand the skills needed for the work and what you have done in the past. Compare to see if it aligns.

"Productivity is never an accident. It is always the result of a commitment to excellence, intelligent planning and focused effort."

~ Paul J. Meyer ~

In this particular situation the candidate herself was wondering if she could do the work. As we dissected her resume, I shared the work I needed with her. Together we identified things she had done. Although the title did not appear to align, as we ran down the tasks and accomplishments, we found the alignment was excellent.

Before you apply for the next level position, look carefully at your resume. Make sure you meet the minimum requirements. Also make sure your past work makes sense in the current context. So I'm not saying to be disingenuous or anything like that. What I am saying is if something aligns, you need to draw the alignment for the hiring manager because they may not figure it out on their own.

Need for Champion Internally

It is extremely important to have a champion internally for an organization.

A lot of folks will use the terms sponsor and champion interchangeably. I would argue they are a very different thing. A champion in an organization is really invested in you as a contributor to the company. They have great passion around you succeeding.

Don't get this confused with someone who likes you. A champion generally has this great passion for you to succeed and you garnering your contribution because it's good for the company. A sponsor is somebody who is invested, but they don't have the passion. They won't necessarily go to the mat to make it happen for you.

In my current position, a recruiter made all the difference in getting me the opportunity. I was willing to accept the position and come in at a lower level. The lady recruiting me really lobbied very hard for me to get the interview. She went to the individual who is our boss today and said she could only have a comfort level if I was allowed to be interviewed.

I most likely was the dark horse in this particular case, but she really lobbied for me. She worked with me on my weaknesses and also made the company understand the contributions I had made inside and outside the company as well. Her passion to champion me was definitely driven by her awareness of what the company needed and what they were trying to achieve.

> *"In order to be a mentor, and an effective one, one must care. You don't have to know how many square miles are in Idaho. You don't need to know the chemical makeup of blood or water. Know what you know and care about the person. Care about what you know and care about the person you're sharing it with."*
>
> ~ May Angelou ~

In a previous situation, I was downsized yet kept in touch with the vice president of the company, Randy. Later, when I was working with someone named Sheryl, this relationship helped. I had applied for a position, but Sheryl did not know me. Through working with Randy, who knew my work, he was able to articulate my value to Sheryl. He was able to explain why I should be hired for the job and not be allowed to walk out the door. Over the years, keeping the connection with Randy allowed me to stay engaged with the organization. Combined with the other techniques I have talked about, he was able to be that champion.

Your champions aren't necessarily always in front of you. It might be somebody who worked with a lot of years ago, but it's somebody who has a passion and recognizes your skill set. They know how you can apply it and make a valuable contribution to the organization.

Champion for Lance

On the subject of championing, a young man I champion comes to mind. His name is Lance. I've talked with Lance on the phone and understand his background. I am clear that he has a tremendous skill set and how he can contribute to my company.

I do not have strong alliances to Lance, but I will tell you, I fought tooth and nail for him. His father and I worked together many years ago, but it's strictly a professional relationship. We aren't really friends, but I know the organization Lance works for and it is a world class organization. My peer in that organization is Ben. I know Lance has a very good reputation with Ben. I got a call from Lance's dad one day and he asked if I can help his kid get a job in North Carolina because he and his wife want to make a move.

I interviewed him on the phone. I didn't have anything for him, but as I looked around my company I did find different positions I could plug him into. I made the introduction because of my passion to bring him on as a team member because I know we can use his skill set at the company.

Championing Lance was a personal experience where I felt strongly about someone who can contribute to my company even though there's not a personal relationship. I had a passion because I believe his skill set will help the company. He recently was hired and is doing a fantastic job.

Do's and Don'ts For Priorities

Do Compromise and Negotiate

Business is a give and take. If you draw a line in the sand and say you aren't going to cross this line at all you will have problems. If you stand and say you aren't going to give on your position at all, people will find you difficult to work with and they won't want to give you a chance.

So, I think you need to hear the other side and come to a compromise through negotiation. It makes a stronger organization. It is the essence of collaboration.

Do Be Honest

Honesty is essential, even when it hurts. Being honest isn't always the easiest thing to do, but it is important. Earlier in my career I found it difficult to be honest because it could hurt people's feelings. In one instance, I was not being totally honest with an employee and she interpreted that she was doing a great job and was about to move up the ladder. I left the impression because I cared about her feelings. By not being completely honest, I created a situation that was more detrimental because now it would be more difficult for this employee to find her gaps and course correct.

Do Know Priorities

Understand what is priority. Generally, what I find folks look at is their vein of work and choose their priorities. Sometimes, what is really the most advantageous is to look across the enterprise. You may say, *"You know, all the work I have been trying to fix is in a "B" category of priority. Someone over here is having trouble getting these couple of "A" category things done. I can deploy some resources and help them."*

Now I know we're not always in a position to do that, but any time we can look with an enterprise perspective, I think it is really important when we consider advancing the organization when it comes to setting priorities.

Do Ask People About Themselves

We all like it when somebody takes an interest in us. As we start to interact with people it helps build your brand as a team player within the organization. People like to know you care and you are connected. It kind of holds people together. You won't know who the people are interacting with you or those you are leading if you don't ask them about themselves.

Do Be Highly Ethical and of Good Character

It's easy for us to point to leaders in the past who have been fine leaders but they have not necessarily been of good character. When this happens their ability to influence coworkers and peers is damaged. It has impaired their ability to lead. I never ever forget character is something you own. It's something you have to build and invest in. If you lose it, it takes a lifetime to rebuild it.

Do Be Flexible

Today we see our business changing on a dime and we have to be flexible. We need to be aware of what is changing and have the ability to make the change.

Do Have a Purpose

We've all been in a meeting where someone is talking just for the sake of talking. To be taken seriously, your attendance has to have a purpose. There must be a purpose for your actions and you have to know what it is you are contributing to the organization. With a purpose you add value and you absolutely want to add value. Then go plug in where you do add value. Whether it's the organization or just your own daily task, you always want to be aware of purpose.

Do Be 85% Aligned with Your Boss

If you want to move up the ladder it is really important you be about eighty-five percent aligned with your boss. You really don't want to be 100% aligned with your boss because you're just replicating exactly what your leadership already knows. What's the value in that? It's the other fifteen percent where you can really influence with a different lens. I always encourage my staff to bring a different opinion to me. The other fifteen percent is so important.

People have asked about only being about twenty percent aligned with their boss. Well, if you have eighty percent different ideas of where the organization should go – your boss may see it as detrimental. I really look for the opportunity to get other ideas from my folks when they find fifteen to twenty percent of my ideas don't align with them.

In my own career the lowest rating I ever had was very helpful to me. It was still a fine rating but on my review it showed I was about eighty five percent aligned with my boss. She and I agreed on those things, while there were a couple of things where we didn't agree. It was really perfect because it shows she is developing me in the way I needed to be developed. It's what made the rating so great.

~~~ ~~~ ~~~ ~~~ ~~~ ~~~ ~~~ ~~~ ~~~ ~~~

Don 't Worry

You know the equation. Worry leads to stress and stress leads to fear. If we find ourselves in a position of fear we are just surviving and not thriving. It's important for us to not worry and to feel confident on where we are so we can move forward.

Don't Be Cruel

We all have pressures in life and it's easy to lash out at folks, particularly when they have a high tolerance for us. It's really important not to be cruel. We need to care about each other in business. As you look at people who move up and are successful in modern business today they typically are not cruel.

Don't Over-Share

I have found some folks share too much information and the result is not good. We all have our personal lives, but we need to keep in mind that it is personal, not business. We are in a work environment and people don't need to know everything about your personal life.

Don't Take a Position for Money

You know money is an important tool to all of us. But as I said earlier, money really has a single time payout for our satisfaction. If you're doing a job you don't enjoy just because of money you'll become miserable. You just won't be able to be as successful as when you look for the right motivators.

5

CONTINUOUS SELF-IMPROVEMENT

This book cannot identify the exact steps you need to take on your journey to continuous self-improvement. Your journey is very personal and unique. However, you will know it when you see it.

The Japanese call it Kaizen, which means improvement or change for the better. For those who practice Kaizen, it is not about a specific event of improvement, it is a philosophy about life. It is a daily process.

> "The good news is that the moment you decide what you know is more important than what you have been taught to believe, you will have shifted gears in your quest for abundance. Success comes from within, not from without.
>
> ~ Ralph Waldo Emerson ~

Companies have tried to adopt the philosophy in total quality management and other initiatives. The same philosophy can be adapted to your personal brand and your desire to hack the corporate ladder.

The Fosbury Flop

Before Dick Fosbury failed to clear the height required for the high jump, everyone had performed the high jump in the same manner. An athlete tossed their body over the bar and crashed into a landing pit on the other side. To soften the blow, the landing pit was filled with wood chips and sawdust. Because of the landing pit material, it was necessary for the jumper to approach the bar face forward.

Fosbury's high school was one of the first to install a foam landing pit. With the new landing environment, he had a crazy idea. He turned his body, arched his back and went over the bar backwards. The foam allowed him to land on his neck/shoulders in a safe way.

The first time he used the technique, a local newspaper ridiculed him as "The World's Laziest High Jumper" and published a photo of him sliding over the bar backwards. But in 1968 he used the technique to win the NCAA championship and qualify for the Olympics. Within 10 years his technique was the standard. For the last 35 years nearly every single Olympic gold medal winner has used the "Fosbury Flop" to succeed.

Self-Improvement Steps

The secret to continuous self-improvement is more about attitude than method. Like the Japanese, it becomes a personal philosophy of your life and career. Here is a few behaviors common to those who adopt this way of life:

- Be open, curious and non-judgmental regarding differing opinions

- Self-reflect and ask for feedback from others

- Identify your individual challenges and seek ways to grow

- Set concrete goals for desired work outcomes and the behaviors required to achieve them

- Be constantly on the lookout for new technical information to use on the job

Setting Yourself Apart

When you are seeking to get to the next level in your job it can be challenging. Across industries and in different experiences the game is going up higher and higher every day. Even within your level of education it is getting more crowded.

> *"Be yourself. Everyone else is taken."*
>
> ~ Oscar Wilde ~

Recent college graduates are so smart and well trained to the value of setting themselves apart. They know it is critical, yet a higher G.P.A. is not what makes them different. These young college grads work hard to put the pieces of the puzzle together to reflect who they are and why it matters to prospective employers.

For me, early in my career I was downsized out of an organization and looked into different jobs. It was clear I couldn't even pay my mortgage based on unemployment and anything else available to me. So I scrambled and found something called Six Sigma. I didn't know what it was. I worked with the hiring manager Sheryl Gates and learned this training offered a fairly rare skill set.

I felt having this new skill set would help me keep my position next time I was faced with a downsize situation. It would give me something else in my tool belt. I interviewed for the position, got hired and got the training.

Since the late ninety's I've been a practitioner of Six Sigma. I am a master black belt now. I found through my career people were very attracted to the rare skill set and training. Six Sigma is pretty pervasive now in business. But in the ninety's it was something making me look different.

Say YES to New Opportunity

In another organization, the company was on the downside and it looked as if we might be actually pulled out of a contract. We all knew the jobs were going away. One day my boss called me and said we don't know what's going to happen with your job. Would you ever move to Europe? I said well sure.

I've found the answer should always be yes. Then if you don't like where it's leading you can always say no.

After I said yes he told me things were going to move relatively quickly. He called me on Monday. We negotiated some things on Tuesday and Wednesday. They made me a final offer on Thursday. I accepted the job, said my goodbyes to everybody on Friday. I packed over the weekend, was on a plane Monday and Tuesday I was in Europe. That's really, really fast...but guess what...people don't do those things. If you do, it sets you apart.

Going to Europe told leadership "This guy's different." They saw I was willing to do things differently and take chances. It was a combination to set me apart from others. When I came back to the United States, leadership was attracted to the fact I had international experience.

Embrace the Unknown

Taking this opportunity to work in Europe provided a multifaceted advantage for me. I remind myself and others to not be afraid of the unknown. It may be scary, for sure, but in the end your company's going to take care of you. We are smart people. We know what to do.

Demonstrate Your Value

"The greatest mistake you can make in life is to be continuously fearing you will make one."

~ Elbert Hubbard ~

One day my CEO came to me with an operational challenge about regulatory organization. Frankly, the company was in hot water. Since the CEO was aware of my background in operations he wanted me to get involved, even though I had nothing to do with the problem or process getting us into the sticky situation. I was in no way accountable for the resulting issues.

He told me he needed my help. I helped.

Many people will say they don't have the skill set or band width to tackle issues outside of their job description and responsibilities. I never shy away from the challenge. I have even "raised my hand" around different challenges. Whether it's my work stream or not, the organization is paying me. I look at the situation as involving the organization's money and I am willing to step in if I can help.

It is a way I differentiate myself as a leader. It gets people's attention. While it sometimes feels like a curse, it's a good thing. The CEO continues to give me high visibility projects that are good for the company. Taking this type of action is also good for my personal growth and personal brand. The opportunities set me aside and help me be perceived as a hero. It may be work nobody else wants to do, but it gets me attention and accolades. It is a powerful way to demonstrate my value.

Determining the Gaps

As you move up the corporate ladder it is important you constantly think about the gaps in your skill and experience.

Start by asking these simple questions:

- What is required by the job I don't currently have?

- What is an area where I need to work to make myself better?

- How can I make a more substantial contribution?

When you are applying for a new position take a careful look at your resume compared to the position description. If you have a gap, figure out what is needed. Do you need training or some other sort of interaction?

In my most recent position, I could not find a position description. The company had not developed a position description for the C-level officer I hope to hold one day. So I actually asked for an appointment with the guy currently in the C-level role. He set down and looked at my resume and said you're missing this and you're missing this and you're missing this. I took notes and am currently working on those gaps. So, when the time comes for me to move to the next level, I will have those gaps filled.

If you can partner with the person on the job it is excellent.

> "We keep moving forward, opening new doors, and doing new things, because we're curious and curiosity keeps leading us down new paths."
>
> ~ Walt Disney ~

Because the person is actually doing it. But if you can only get the position description, look at the comparison and work on closing any gaps. You may need formal training or some other type of work experience.

In my situation, the C-level executive told me I didn't have enough volunteer board experience and helped me get plugged into some volunteer boards. This type of information is very important, but it's not something you're going to pick up in a textbook.

Independent Skills Assessments

Never be afraid to use independent skills assessments and training. Once, when I was applying for a position, I learned the hiring manager wanted someone who had good PowerPoint skills. Even though using PowerPoint was not part of my job and I already had fairly good skills with the software, I wanted to be better. I took an independent skills assessment to determine my current level of proficiency. Once I knew where I should start training I went out and found a 2-day PowerPoint course at one of the local learning centers.

During the interview process I was able to show the hiring manager some of my skills and got offered the job. She commented that apparently she and I were the only people in the company to know how to do this level of PowerPoint work. It gave us a valuable bonding point. She's given me some assignments and while my job is not about sitting down and putting PowerPoints together, if you're the only person with the skill set and the boss needs it...it's a good thing to be able to do the work. The independent skills assessment were quite valuable.

Do's and Don'ts For Self-Improvement

Do Seek Knowledge

Any one person who feels they have all the answers is absolutely incorrect. This is particularly true as you move up the corporate ladder. You have to be willing to say you don't know the answer and promise to get back to them.

When you look at the great leaders in the world, I find they have surrounded themselves with people who have a greater knowledge than they do in certain areas. Anyone who moves up the corporate ladder comes from that place. I think if you don't have the ability to say, *"Hey, I don't know the answer. Help me,"* you're limiting your ability to grow.

Do Have More than One Discipline

Discipline can go across several areas as a generalist or you can be a subject matter expert in a few areas and go deep into the discipline. What you can't do is just go half way deep in one discipline because it will make you average. You know how I feel about average, right?

If you choose to go deep you need to look at a few disciplines. I really have three disciplines to feel proud about. They are operations management, process improvement and risk management. When I look at those three things, I'm able to drive efficiencies through operations because I know how the operations work. Then I can actually couple those outcomes with my risk register. As we see risks emerge, we can avoid going back afterwards to say our performance was poor because we have a risk in this area. We can actually see the risk coming down the road and course correct before we get there. This is one example of how my disciplines have been applied to my own career and life.

Do Be of Good Humor

We spend many more hours in the workplace than our folks and grand folks did. Having a good humor helps connect you with people. It makes it a more enjoyable place to be. It's important to keep humor alive in our work.

Do Be Clear

I've had to work on this one. I've learned I need to probably be a little less diplomatic and more direct which leads to greater clarity. It's no good for any of us to walk away hearing a different message than what was delivered just because I was trying to be nice. It doesn't mean we should be rude or inappropriate. However, you always want to be clear what you're trying to say so both parties can be successful in executing against the purpose of the conversation. If you do that people will respect your opinion and respect your stance and point of view.

Do Take Chances

Don't be afraid. People who live in a cocoon, and avoid taking chances, will miss opportunities. Recently I was out of the country in a place with a reputation of not being the safest country. When I was there I found out about the Pulse Nightclub attack in Orlando. It made me realize we may think we're safe and we try to stay in this cocoon, but it's not necessarily true. Never be afraid to take chances.

Do Know Your Skill Set

Your skill set ties into knowing who you are. Knowing who you are is more about your character. Interpersonal abilities are your skill set. None of us know everything by any means. So, when you look at your skill set, you can either be viewed in a general sense or it can be very deep in a specific sense.

You need the inventory to know where you can contribute within the business organization.

Do Have Humility

Being humble is important to climbing the corporate ladder. I think back to one of my first experiences with a peer who became a leader. I started my illustrious career at McDonalds at the age of sixteen. A peer who worked there got promoted. It was interesting because she lost her humility. In reality, she ended up driving people away. She was not a nice person to work with and I definitely tie her results back to humility.

When you are given a position of leadership, someone has faith in you. They are trying to instill leadership in you. This is a place where we need to be humble and certainly not arrogant.

~~~~ ~~~~ ~~~~ ~~~~ ~~~~ ~~~~ ~~~~ ~~~~ ~~~~

Don't Apply for Every Job

I think of a young man who was in an entry level position. It turned out he was in my reporting line and I learned he applied for every single job. For any job that was open he would put his name in for it. He became a joke and nobody would pay him any attention. This is somebody in his early twenties and he is applying for Chief Financial Officer without any educational background to support his application.

Don't apply for the sake of applying. Instead, apply because there is a need for the company and you can fulfill the need. The worst thing that could happen if you apply and you're not qualified, is you actually get the job and then fail. It's important to look at the qualifications and make a determination around whether you are a fit.

Don't Over Market Yourself

This "don't" kind of goes with some of the do's mentioned earlier about your skill set and knowing who you are. When you run into an individual who over markets themselves it looks like you are saying you can do everything under the sun. None of us really knows everything. It shows up as over marketing and reflects a lack of confidence. Be mindful about how you market your skill set.

Don't Lie

This "don't" ties in with being of good character. If you lie you will be found out. When you destroy your credibility you really impair your ability to lead. You impair your ability to contribute because people don't trust you.

Don't Make Unreasonable Demands

Unreasonable demands is coupled with putting pressure on folks. We all have productivity standards to meet. We have our name on the bottom line of something. When we are faced with unreasonable demands it just has a negative impact that leads to worry…stress…fear and then we're just trying to survive. Right? Not thrive.

6

3-POINT MANAGEMENT PHILOSOPHY

My management philosophy can be reduced to three management tools. I have managed using these really super simple tools and found them to be super effective.

1. **Set Expectations:**

   We cannot expect people to achieve success if they don't know where they're going. If they don't know what the boss wants, it is impossible to meet the boss's expectations.

2. **Give Folks the Tools They Need:**

   Without the tools needed to accomplish the task, people cannot meet your expectations. A manager who worked for me came back after some time off and scolded one of his employees because she had not completed a presentation.

   What I learned later is he hadn't made it clear what he expected and wasn't explicit about when he wanted it completed. She was a younger employee and he wanted a PowerPoint. She hadn't been trained in PowerPoint so she didn't have the skills. How could he have expected her to be successful?

3. **Hold People Accountable**:

   Now, accountability is a two-way street. So if I've invested in you and have told you what I need…I've invested to make sure you have what you need to deliver it…you need to deliver it. It's part of your accountability.

My part of the accountability is the first two things. If I'm not clear or don't give you what you need to do the job, I can't hold you accountable. The example used in the second point where my manager was holding his employee accountable, he didn't fulfill his part...items one and two. So three could never occur.

This very simple 3 –point management philosophy is a formula to make you a better manager. You'll have more success and it will absolutely help you move to the next level quicker.

ROBERT T. GOFOURTH

AFTERWORD

You Made It! Well, almost!

Congratulations! You have made it to the end of the book. There are lots of things that you should know by now. Perhaps one of the most important observation that you have made is this: The business world is about relationships. Rob has done a masterful job laying out a blueprint to shape and build the most important relationship that you will ever have...that being the relationship with yourself. What he has shared is powerful. This is the kind of information that most leaders wished they had known before attempting to build a career in corporate America, including me. This is the kind of insight that will make the difference between a mildly successful career and a wildly successful career. Success comes from the inside out. No one can give you the magic formula. You must be willing to find the courage to dig deep to discover the leader in you. You have the framework now, but there is more much more than you can do to get the most out of this book.

Personal Change: Using What You've Learned

Perhaps you have heard that knowledge is power. If so, may I offer a different perspective, knowledge in and of itself is not powerful. Knowledge only becomes powerful when we make a choice to put it to use. So, the question and the invitation before you is ... "what will you do with all this newfound knowledge"? How will you build your own Kaizen (your plan of action to improve your leadership capabilities by applying what you have learned?). Your destiny to higher levels of success begins with a question...do you have the discipline to apply the learning. There is a great change management model that a good friend, Greg Magennis shared with me a few years ago. The model is by a man named James O. Prochaska. Prochaska is a Professor of Psychology and director of the Cancer Prevention Research Center at the University of Rhode Island and developer of the Transtheoretical Model of Behavior Change beginning in 1977. Prochaska earned his B.A. in Psychology at Wayne State University in 1964, followed by his M.A. and Ph.D. Degrees both at Wayne State. He is the author or co-author of over 250 handwritten publications on the dynamics of behavioral change.

(source: http://www.cpe.vt.edu/gttc/presentations/8eStagesofChange.pdf)

His model suggests that there are eight steps to making change that sticks... The Stages of Change The stages of change are:

- ✓ Pre-contemplation (Not yet acknowledging that there is a problem behavior that needs to be changed)

- ✓ Contemplation (Acknowledging that there is a problem but not yet ready or sure of wanting to make a change)

- ✓ Preparation/Determination (Getting ready to change)

- ✓ Action/Willpower (Changing behavior)

- ✓ Maintenance (Maintaining the behavior change)

- ✓ Relapse (Returning to older behaviors and abandoning the new changes)

Beliefs, Habits, Behaviors and Patterns

Where are you? Do you understand that achieving success in corporate America takes more than showing up daily? It even takes more than showing up daily and doing a good job. It takes a personal strategy. What Rob has written represents the key components (through his do's and don'ts) of a personal strategy. I hope and I know that Rob does too, that you are in the action of building new capabilities and behaviors. How can you stay in this zone or the maintenance zone and not lapse back into old behaviors? The answer is simple - practice on a daily basis. In fact, develop daily habits that you know will reinforce the learning and help you to achieve higher levels of success. Have you ever wondered what successful people do on a daily basis? I have. In fact, I have studied many successful leaders. Let me share just a few examples of how they maintain a high level of success. Many of these items have been covered in detail in the book but let me add a few more. Successful people have a vision. They also know their strengths. They look for the intersection between their strengths, their capabilities, and the organization's needs. This is what we as coaches refer to as the "sweet spot". When you are in this space you are positioned to add the greatest value possible to the organization. Value and impact are two words that you should think about on a daily basis. How can you add more value? How can you expand your impact? Leaders are not leaders because of a title. They are leaders because they add value and impact, unleash talent in others and foster environments where possibilities are endless. The next thing that I tell every coaching client that I take on is to make a weekly appointment with themselves. I call it "whitespace". Whitespace is where you think. It is time to reflect, to study, to build course correction plans when things go wrong. Successful leaders study the marketplace. They know how their value aligns with the companies' goals and they are ahead of the curve in adopting behaviors because they study the trends.

Successful leaders are also very intentional. They don't believe in waiting for opportunities to come to them, they are creators of opportunities. More than anything they are disciplined. They remain committed to personal growth even in the midst of chaos. They treat themselves in many ways like athletes. Athletes don't like to exercise every day. Just ask a few. But what they like is the success that comes from exercising and preparing to demonstrate their craft. They are able to drown out the noise and naysayers. They remain focused on the target. But they also know something else. They know that they absolutely, positively cannot do it alone. They surround themselves with people who will challenge their thinking. Remember Rob shared that I challenge his thought process. If you are surrounded by people who are always telling you how good you are, it is time for some new friends. People who care about you aren't afraid to have the courageous conversations with you. Rob referred to these people as "truth tellers" I love that phrase. I have lots of truth tellers in my life. Truth tellers aren't brutal. They speak in a spirit of love. They tell you the truth because they know that's what is best for you.

Other things that successful leaders do is to be mindful of how they process the world around them. There is so much violence, evil, and bad things happening in the world. How does a great leader avoid succumbing to thoughts of doom and gloom? They learn to trust themselves. They believe in themselves and in the goodness of others. They look back at life and they find out how they made it through the storms of life. The insight that they obtain shapes their leadership principles. You might not have ever done this exercise but as you build your own strategy, consider stepping back, reflecting and capturing the 10 most defining moments in your life. You will be amazed at what you have already achieved in life. You will be shocked when you realize that you have been managing change all your life. You will be surprised when you realize that you are resilient and resourceful. You will wonder how you didn't know these things about yourself before. You see that's what Rob is inviting you to do. He is inviting you to discover yourself.

This is obviously not an exhaustive list. Successful leaders have other daily habits that add to their ability to not just survive, but thrive. Like exercise. I would hurt people if I didn't exercise. You must have some way of releasing the stress. Or, like Rob said it will turn to fear. And what is fear? Fear is just faith focused on the wrong thing. That's my definition. So think long and hard about what you believe, what habits and behaviors that you should keep and let go of, and think about the patterns that are shaping your life for better. Hang on to those, let the bad ones go and develop new ones on a daily basis.

It's time to Stretch Yourself

One of my favorite sayings is "go big or go home". It is related to sports and I don't honestly even know where or when I first heard it. It translates to "do your best", "give your all", "aim for excellence". I grew up in the deep south during a very difficult time in American history. I grew up in segregation. It was a turmoil filled time. It was also a time of opportunity. People tried to shape my dreams for me by saying things like - I should go to trade school after high school. I would say that I wanted to run a company someday.

In response, I would receive comments like "black women can't run companies". I refused to listen. I refused to give my power away. You know we give our power away by allowing others to determine how far we can go in life. My mother use to say "as long as you do your best" there isn't anything else that anyone can ask for. She used to also say there is no such word as "can't". I have been holding onto those words all my life. Now as Founder and CEO of my own company I look back and wonder, what would or could I have achieved if only someone would have had the courage to whisper in my ear the secrets to success in the business world.

I am grateful to Rob for his willingness to demonstrate vulnerability. In fact, great leaders are not only willing to be vulnerable, they embrace vulnerability. And, so should you.

If you don't have clarity yet, don't be disappointed. This is a journey, nor a marathon or a 100 yard dash. Stretch yourself to dream more than others think is wise. If you shoot for the moon and you only get a star that is more than most people will ever achieve in several life times. If a little country girl like me can find a way to fulfill her dreams with no blueprint, imagine what you can do now that you have the blueprint.

Don't put this book away. Keep it and use it, refer to it, cry on it, smile with it in your hands. Feel the power!

One Final Thing

I simply cannot close out my thoughts without adding one final comment. GIVE! Be a leader who gives. Give something away daily. Sow seeds of goodness. Say something nice to someone else every day. Light your family up. Be an encourager. Remember people want to be around people who are positive, see possibilities, think outside the box and yes, succeed! As you learn the secrets, pay it forward. Give and you will get.

I wish you nothing but SUCCESS!

Trudy Bourgeois

Specializing in Leadership Development for Women and People of Color
Author | Speaker | Change Agent
The Center for Workforce Excellence

WorkforceExcellence.com

ROBERT T. GOFOURTH

ABOUT THE AUTHOR

Robert is a business leader with great passion for developing talent and high performing teams. He believes that as a society we must look beyond the traditional approaches to business and change the way we think. We now have five generations in the workforce. Each unique with its own set of strengths and challenges.

Originally from Lake Placid located in south central Florida, Robert currently lives in Durham, NC and thinks it is a gem of a city. After graduating University of Florida, his career has taken him around the world. These assignments have given him the opportunity to lead teams from a variety of different cultures and countries.

When not working, he enjoys traveling, public speaking and giving back to community. Robert sits on several charitable and professional boards. He believes that we all must "Pay it Forward".

Follow Robert T. Gofourth on Social Media:

Twitter: @Robgofourth

Facebook: facebook.com/RobertTGofourth

Instagram: instagram.com/Robgofourth1

LinkedIn: linkedin.com/in/rob-gofourth-b21b813

Snap Chat: Robgofourth1

Email: robgofourth@gmail.com

Website: www.HackTheCorporateLadder.com

www.ingramcontent.com/pod-product-compliance
Lightning Source LLC
Chambersburg PA
CBHW071819200526
45169CB00018B/467